HEAVEN AND MIRTH®

David

God's Rock Star

AND
OTHER BIBLE STORIES TO TICKLE YOUR SOUL

by Mike Thaler

Illustrated by Dennis Adler

*Equiping Kids
for Life*

A Faith Parenting Guide can be found on page 32.

Dedicated to
John and Sue Guldseth,
God's love in their hearts.
Mike

Faith Kids™ is an imprint of
Cook Communications, Colorado Springs, Colorado 80918
Cook Communications, Paris, Ontario
Kingsway Communications, Eastbourne, England

DAVID: GOD'S ROCK STAR
© 2000 by Mike Thaler for text and Dennis Adler for illustrations

Faith Kids™ is a registered trademark of Cook Communications Ministries.

HEAVEN AND MIRTH® is a registered trademark of Mike Thaler.

Published in association with the literary agency of Alive Communications, Inc.,
1465 Kelly Johnson Blvd., Suite 320, Colorado Springs CO 80920.

Edited by Jeannie Harmon
Design by Clyde Van Cleve

First hardcover printing, 2000
Printed in Singapore
04 03 02 01 00   5 4 3 2 1

Letter from the Author

Taking this opportunity, I would like to share with you how this book came about. Born sixty-two years ago, I have been a secular children's book author most of my life. I was also content to have a fast-food relationship with God from the drive-by window. At the age of sixty, I came into the banquet by inviting Jesus Christ into my heart. Since then my life has been a glorious feast. These stories are part of that celebration.

One night I sat and watched a sincere grandfather trying to read Bible stories to his squirming grandchildren. I asked him, "Aren't there any humorous retellings of Bible stories that are vivid and alive for kids?" He rolled his eyes and said, "This is it." The kids rolled their eyes, too.

This made me sad, for the Bible is the most exciting, valuable, and alive book I know—as is its Author. So I went into my room, with this in mind, and wrote "Noah's Rainbow."

Since then God has anointed me with sixty stories that fire my imagination and light up my heart. They are stories which, I hope, are filled with the joy, love, and spirit of the Lord.

Mike Thaler
West Linn 1998

Nuggets from Goldie the miner prophet:
"It's Never Too Late to Eat Right."

Author's Note

I have conscientiously tried to follow each story in word and spirit as found in the Bible. But in some cases, for the sake of storytelling, I have taken minor liberties and added small details. I pray for your understanding in these instances.

The Tower of Babble
The Semantic Titanic

AFTER THE FLOOD,
Noah had a clean new world.
He and his three sons—
Shem, Ham, and Japheth—
began populating the earth again.
In a few generations,
they were one big happy family.
They all lived near each other
and spoke the same language.

"It's a big world out there," said God.
"Let's spread out a little, fellas."

But no one wanted to leave home,
and besides they were into urban sprawl.
They had learned how to make bricks,
so they built a development
called Shiner City.

If one neighbor sneezed,
the whole block would say,
"God bless you!"

They were feeling good
about building, so they decided
to take on a bigger project —
a giant brick tower
that would go up into the sky.
They would name it after their
great-great-grandfather:
the SHEMPIRE STATE BUILDING.

They started to build and the higher they went,
the more important they felt.
When the tower rose near the clouds,
they began to feel like God Himself.

When someone would sneeze,
they'd say, "We bless you!"

"Hey," said God. **"This is a bad trend."**

So He immediately blew the whistle on the whole project.

That night He gave everyone a different language.
And when they came to work
the next morning,
one person said, "Hello,"
another said, *"Bon Jour,"*
a third said, "𝕲𝖚𝖙𝖊𝖓 𝖒𝖔𝖗𝖌𝖊𝖓,"
and the others said, "Καλι μερα."
Needless to say, no one understood anyone else,
and they didn't get much done that day.
They just languished around.

And that night when they all went home,
they packed their bags and moved as far away
from each other as they could get.

"That's more like it," smiled God.
"Now you're talkin' My language."

THE END

Nuggets from Goldie, the miner prophet:

"If you build up yourself instead of God, you won't get off the ground."

For the real story, read Genesis 11.

Joseph
Papa's Pet

ISRAEL HAD TWELVE SONS.
His favorite was Joseph,
who was definitely *Papa's pet*.

All the other boys wore
hand-me-down coats.
But Joseph's coat was
brand new and
of the latest fashion.

He was also the only one
allowed to sleep late
in the morning.
While the other boys
were up working,
Joseph was down dreaming.
He was dreaming
about all his brothers
working for him.
They did not like this.
In fact, they talked about ways
to get rid of him.

"We could put him in the wine press
and make Joseph juice."

"We could throw him in front of a camel train."

"We could simply sell 'im."

And one day they did.

They sold him to be a slave
in a land called Egypt.

10

Joseph was bought by a rich man
named Potiphar,*
and soon he became
the favorite slave in the house.
Then all the other servants
resented him.
They called him *Potiphar's pet,*
and they plotted ways
to get rid of him.

"We could put him in a wine press."

"We could throw him in front of a camel train."

"We could say he made a pass at the boss's wife."

And one day they did.

Potiphar got peeved and threw Joseph in jail,
where he became the *Jailer's pet.*
He would wander around prison
interpreting everyone's dreams,
and he soon became the *Prisoner's pet.*

*pronounced Pot-of-fur

11

So when one prisoner,
   Pharaoh's head butler,
      was released,
         he told Pharaoh about Joseph.

      "This guy's really nice,
         and he interprets dreams."

      Now Pharaoh was having
         some weird dreams,
         so he sent for Joseph,
         who told him what they meant,
         and Joseph became *Pharaoh's pet*.
      But nobody minded because
         he saved everyone from starving,
         and then he was *Egypt's pet*.

   One day his brothers came before him
      asking for food.
   They didn't recognize him,
      for he was all dressed up
   in the latest Egyptian fashions, and wore pyramittens.
   When they came back to ask him for seconds,
      he told them who he was.

They cried, had a big family reunion,
and they all moved in.

When they heard about his many good fortunes,
they unanimously agreed,
that surely, Joseph was *God's pet.*

THE END

Nuggets from Goldie, the miner prophet:
"Clothes can't make the man, if righteousness is out of fashion."

For the real story read Genesis 37–47.

David

God's Rock Star!

T HE ARMY OF THE PHILISTINES STOOD ON A HILL.
Across the way, crouched the army of the Israelites,
and between them stood an empty valley.

Nobody moved until the giant warrior Goliath
stepped forward.
He was as tall as a statue.
Ten men could lie down in his shadow,
and you could take a bath in his helmet.

"Oh, men of Israel,"
    he thundered.
      "Why do you just stand
        on the mountain like trees?
         Send forth a warrior to meet me
          in combat and the winner's tribe
           shall have their sandals shined by the losers."

        "Any volunteers?" asked King Saul.

         His whole army was shaking like leaves
         and they all took a step backwards.

          "Well, we'll let you know tomorrow,"
         shouted Saul, running into his tent.

          For forty days, Goliath strode forward
         and shouted his challenge.
          And each day he drove the nail of fear deeper
         into their wooden hearts,
        till hardly a man could move or speak.

On the forty-first day, young David arrived,
delivering a pizza to his older brothers.
And when he heard the bluster of Goliath,
he said to the fear-rooted men around him,
"Who is this blowhard
to threaten the army of the Lord?"

"Shhh," cried his brothers,
"he might hear you."

"I don't care if this bean-brained
bully hears me," shouted David.

All the men backed away.

"I'll go out and deal with this wide-load warrior myself."

"But, David," pleaded Saul, "you are but a youth, not even shaving yet.
How can you possibly do battle against this giant?"

"My king," smiled David, "when you stand with God,
you stand tall. And besides, I'm into rock and roll."

"Well, take my armor and my sword," said Saul.
"My king," smiled David, "I have the armor of God."
And picking up five smooth stones,
David strolled out to meet Goliath.

When Goliath looked down
and saw little David, he laughed so hard
the leaves blew off the trees.

"Why do they send a flea to fight a lion?
A mouse to threaten an elephant?
I will squash you under my sandal."

"Not so fast, big boy, you've got a sword
but I've got the Lord," said David,
loading a stone into his sling shot
and swinging it over his head.
"Cannot a flea bite a lion,
and a mouse scare an elephant?"
While Goliath was thinking it over,
David loosed the stone and it struck
Goliath square on the forehead.

"Ouch!" he moaned
as he fell to earth with a *CRASH!*
David climbed on top of the giant
and drew Goliath's sword.

"Sorry, big boy, this is the only way I can get ahead in this story."
And with that he severed Goliath's surprised noggin
from his unhappy body, and held it up for all to see.

"I think our welcome has worn out here,"
shouted the Philistines, and they all ran away.

"Knock, knock," said David.

"Who's there?" answered the army of the Israelites.

"Goliath," said David.

"Goliath, who?" yelled the army.

"Don't Go-lieth down now," shouted David.
"Get those Philistines!"

So the army chased the Philistines all the way back home.

"Boy," said Saul, "I'm really impressed.
How would you like to marry one of my daughters
and have a steady job in my army?"

"Sure," said David.

"But tell me," asked Saul,
"how did you do it?
Goliath is stone cold dead."

"Well," smiled David,
"all things are possible
when God is your rock."

THE END

Nuggets from Goldie, the miner prophet:
"When God is on your side, you don't need any backup."

For the real story read 1 Samuel 17.

Solomon
Too Many Wives Spoil the Chef

Solomon had 700 wives
and 300 concubines.*
Now it's true, that's a lot of tax deductions,
but it also is a lot of trouble.
Just remembering all their birthdays
was a full-time job.
And forget anniversaries.
But the worst part was
most of his wives
believed in other gods
—big gods, little gods,
gods with heads of monkeys,
gods with the feet of chickens.

*Concubines are backup wives, more like dates than mates.

Every other day was a religious holiday:
Shish Kebab's birthday, Cinca de Molech,
  Sacred Hawkins' Day, Super Baal Sunday . . .

  Soon Solomon didn't have time
   to honor the God Almighty,
      the God of his father, David.

         This miffed God a lot,
           so God spoke to Solomon,
             "Solomon, once you were wise,
               but now you're a wise guy.
                 You have a bad attitude.
                 You have broken
                   my commandments,
                     not followed my decrees,
                     and you don't keep
                     your room clean.
                     Because of this,
                       I will tear your kingdom
                       away from you.
                       But because your dad
                       was a good guy,
                       I'll wait till you die."

"Sounds fair to me," sighed Solomon.

But God didn't make
the rest of Solomon's life easy.
In fact, it poured
during the remainder
of his reign.
Besides going into counseling
with all his wives and concubines,
Solomon had to fight many adversaries.
Finally, after twenty years of stress,
he went to an early tomb
and finally rested
next to his dead dad, David.

THE END

Nuggets from Goldie, the miner prophet:
"Life is easier with one God and one wife."

For the real story read 1 Kings 11.

Job

Did You Ever Have One of Those Days?

Job had it made.
He had wealth, health, and family.
He had camels, cows, sheep, and donkeys.
In fact, he was the richest dude in the land of Uz.
But of all the things he had,
he treasured his love of God most.

Job prayed and prayed, and never strayed.
He was an overachiever true believer.
And God was truly proud of him.
In fact, God would brag about Job to all the angels,
and even to the Devil.

"Big deal," said the Devil.
"Sure he's grateful. Look at all You've given him.
Teacher's pet! I bet if You took away any of it,

25

Job would sing a different tune."

"You're on," declared God,
"Take away whatever you want, and we'll just see!"
God had a lot of confidence in Job.

So the Devil went to work. He took away all Job's camels,
all Job's cows, all Job's donkeys and all Job's sheep.
But when Job found out,
he just praised the name of the Lord.

"Easy come, easy go," said Job.

"See," smiled God, **"I told ya so."**

"We'll see," hissed the Devil,
"I'm just warming up."
So the Devil blew down Job's house,
killing all his children,
and all his servants.

When Job got home
and saw what had happened,
he tore his clothes
and shaved his head.
Then he fell to the ground
and praised the Lord.

He cried, "Naked came I into the world,
and naked I will go out.
All things flow from the Lord.
Blessed be the name of the Lord."

"You see," said God,
beaming with pride.

"I don't see anything,"
blustered the Devil.
"Give me a little skin.
He only cares about his own hide.
If we struck *his* flesh, he'd sing a different song."

"Go ahead," said God, **"be my guest.
Just don't kill 'im."**

"I'm going to enjoy this,"
smiled Satan,
rubbing his hands together.
So he took away Job's health.
He gave him a horrible case
of athlete's foot.

"Praise the Lord," sang Job
as he sprinkled on foot powder.

He gave him dandruff.
"Praise the Lord," sang Job
as he shampooed his hair.

Then he gave him horrible boils
all over his body.

"Oh," cried Job, "I wish I was dead!"

"Now we're getting somewhere,"
grinned the Devil.
"We'll see," said God,
"he hasn't cursed Me yet."

As the days progressed,
Satan gave Job one devil of a time.
Job was in constant pain
twenty-four hours a day.
He couldn't stand, he couldn't sit,
he couldn't lie down.
He couldn't even kneel before God.

"Take me, O Lord,
I wish I was never born."

"Progress," snickered the Devil,
clapping his hands.
Then to make things worse,

the Devil sent three stooges to comfort Job.
"How's it going?" asked Harry,
slapping Job on the back.

"Ouch!" wailed Job.

"Are we havin' a bad day?" mocked Surly.

"You know, Job, it could be worse," joked Schmoe.

"How?" cried Job in great pain.

"It could have happened to us,"
they all laughed, falling down on
the ground.
"God is just having
on-the-Job training,"
they chortled.

Suddenly God thundered
down from a storm,
**"Did you ever
wake up the sun?
Have you ever
given the song birds tunes?
Have you ever
painted a butterfly?
What do you know?"**

29

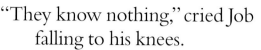

"They know nothing," cried Job
falling to his knees.
"You're number one, primo uno,
You make it all happen,
and whatever You do
is fine with me."

"Get up Job," said God.
"For your faithfulness,
I will restore your health,
wealth, and family.
And since you have been
such a good sport,
I will double all
that you had before."

Then God turned to Harry,
Surly, and Schmoe,
"And, as for you three stooges,
for bugging my true servant Job,
I'm going to make you
have to earn your living
the rest of your days
by acting silly
and falling down."

So Job lived happily to the ripe old age of 140,
and surrounded by his great, great, great, grandchildren,
watched many replays of the films
made by his three friends.

THE END

Nuggets from Goldie, the miner prophet:
"In every cloud, God is the silver lining."

For the real story, read Job 1–42

HEAVEN AND MIRTH®

David
God's Rock Star

Age: 6 and up

Life Issue: Learning to have confidence in God will give us courage in tough circumstances.

Spiritual Building Block: Confidence

Learning Styles

Help your child learn about confidence in the following ways:

Sight: View a video version of the story of David and Goliath. Why did David believe that God would help him win the battle over Goliath? How had God helped David defeat his enemies in the past? What battles do we fight today? How do we know that God will be there when the going gets tough?

Sound: Talk to your child about the meaning of confidence. Confidence is a feeling of security based on faith and trust. Who do we have confidence in to help us when we need help? (Examples: policeman, crossing guard, pastor, doctor, nurse, teacher, etc.). Can we have confidence in God? Why?

Touch: With the help of family members, set up a mini-obstacle course in your living room. Then blindfold your child and let him or her find a way through the course, trying to avoid obstacles. When the child has had some difficulty doing this alone, have family members direct the child safely through the maze by giving vocal directions. God directs us through the maze of our life and we can have confidence that He will take us through safely.